From
Fiber
to
Fine Art

Museum
of
Fine Arts
Boston

Larry Salmon

Catherine Kvaraceus

Matthew X. Kiernan

D1501590

Foreword

The exhibition "From Fiber to Fine Art" is held in celebration of the official founding of the Department of Textiles. Originally part of the Department of Decorative Arts, it became established as a separate entity in 1930. By that time, however, some of the collections had already resided more than fifty years within the walls of the Museum.

It is fitting that this publication be dedicated to the memory of Miss Gertrude Townsend. Appointed assistant in charge of textiles in 1919, she became keeper of textiles and later the first curator of the department. Even after her retirement in 1959, she continued to be active as curator emerita, a position she held until her death last year.

"From Fiber to Fine Art" was planned in order to give the public an idea of the scope of the Museum's textile collections, their wide range, their exquisite quality and inexhaustible variety. This is the accumulated result of more than a hundred years of close cooperation between generous donors, knowledgeable collectors, and expert professionals. Spanning many centuries and including textiles from cultures of all the continents of the world, our textile collection is a perfect reflection of the universality of the Museum. We hope that it will continue to grow and flourish.

JAN FONTEIN
Director

This publication is supported by a grant from Fieldcrest Mills, Inc.

2

Introduction

The Museum of Fine Arts, Boston, is fortunate to have one of the most comprehensive representations of the textile arts in the United States. The preeminence of the textile and costume holdings is due chiefly to the people who supported their acquisition — the donors, trustees, and professional staff members who worked so diligently from the very beginning to form the outstanding collections now in the Museum. The following brief history identifies the major figures responsible for the growth of the department and its collections and illustrates a diverse selection of the most important textile and costume acquisitions.

When the Museum was incorporated in 1870, Boston was the center for the United States' textile industry. Moreover, the desire to elevate the quality of industrially produced objects was growing here as in Europe at that time, a concern that led to various "arts and crafts" movements toward the end of the nineteenth century. It was natural, therefore, that the Museum's founders viewed as essential the formation of a collection of textiles, to provide the manufacturers access to well-selected historical examples of design. In doing so, the Boston Museum was following the lead of several European textile-producing centers such as London, Krefeld (Germany), and Lyons (France).

With this priority established, the second object accessioned by the Museum was a textile, a Flemish tapestry depicting an allegorical scene of Victory (cat. no. 20). This tapestry, donated in 1871 by Ida Deacon, had once graced the art-filled South End home of her father, Edward Preble Deacon.[1]

The Boston Athenaeum was a great supporter of the fledgling Museum of Fine Arts, placing much of its art collection on deposit in the original museum building in Copley Square when it opened in July 1876. To enlarge this collection it purchased a number of textiles for the Museum at the 1876 Philadelphia Exposition, including a Brussels tapestry, *The Assumption of the Virgin* (cat. no. 13), silk weavings, and ecclesiastical vestments. The money for these purchases came from the insurance on Col. T.B. Lawrence's armor collection, bequeathed to the Athenaeum but tragically destroyed by fire in 1872.[2] In 1877 Alessandro Castellani, the Italian art dealer from whom the textiles had been bought at the Philadelphia Exposition, gave the first costume to enter the collection, a richly patterned eighteenth-century Italian or French dress (cat. no. 31).

Funds for the purchase of textiles were seldom available throughout the early decades of the Museum's history, but the collections grew steadily, nevertheless, through the generosity of many local donors. Chief among these were J.W. Paige and Mrs. George W. Wales, who gave their collections of laces (see cat. nos. 23, 24, and 25), silk weavings, and embroideries. Other important early gifts were a group of forty-seven pre-Columbian Peruvian textiles, given in 1878 by Edward W. Hooper, and the world-renowned Indian pictorial carpet (cat. no. 47), a gift in 1893 in the name of Frederick L. Ames. The architect H.H. Richardson had personally chosen this carpet in 1887 for a house he had designed for Mr. and Mrs. Ames, and he received support in his choice from William Morris, head of England's arts and crafts movement, who wrote upon examining it, "… it is a very rare and fine work of art: it belongs to the highest class of this kind of wares, of which necessarily very few specimens are left, and it is a noble example of that class."[3]

By 1879 the Museum possessed a sufficient number of textiles to require a special gallery for their exhibition. The collections continued to grow, however, and only a small selection could be placed on view at one time, the rest being kept in storage. Loan exhibitions of textiles were also held on occasion, among them an exhibition of laces and embroideries in 1878, one of embroideries in 1883, and two others of fans and shoes in 1892. In early 1893 Frank Gair Macomber, a Boston insurance man and collector, organized a

---

1. In a letter of February 7, 1871, from Ida Deacon to Martin Brimmer, president of the Museum's board of trustees, Miss Deacon wrote: "It is my wish to present it to the future Art Museum, as a memorial of my Father, who, had he lived, would doubtless, with his great love of Art, have been foremost among you in promoting this noble work."

2. *Annual Report*, Museum of Fine Arts, Boston, 1873, p. 7. With Mrs. Lawrence's approval, the trustees of the Athenaeum had earmarked this money to be "devoted to the purchase of works of art for the Museum [of Fine Arts]."

3. Letter dated July 11, 1887, from William Morris to H.H. Richardson.

pioneering exhibition of tapestry weavings, the largest and most varied ever held up to that time in the United States. Including weavings dating from the Early Christian era to the nineteenth century, the exhibition featured an early sixteenth-century Flemish tapestry, *The Destruction of the Egyptians in the Red Sea* (acc. no. 95.1), which was subsequently purchased by the Museum in 1895.

Through the end of the nineteenth century, the emphasis remained more on the acquisition of a broad range of textiles to represent the industrial arts than on individual masterpieces. This was the collecting philosophy of Denman Waldo Ross, a professor of design at Harvard University and Museum trustee from 1895 to 1935. His aesthetic criteria knew no bounds of time, place, or medium, and his gifts enriched virtually every department of the Museum. Dr. Ross began in 1890 a pattern of giving textiles that was to continue for over forty years, and he was more responsible than any other donor for shaping the collection as it exists today.

Among the most important areas represented by Denman Ross's gifts are those of so-called Coptic textiles from Egypt and early Near Eastern silk weavings (see cat. nos. 3 and 5). Most of these came to the Museum between 1893 and 1920, when the Egyptian burial grounds were just beginning to be excavated. Dr. Ross also presented the Museum with pre-Columbian Peruvian embroideries and weavings (see cat. no. 60), as well as a number of complete Colonial Peruvian tapestry weavings (see cat. no. 62). Because of his gifts in this latter area, the Museum of Fine Arts possesses today the largest group of complete Colonial Peruvian weavings in the world. Dr. Ross also gave quantities of European, Persian, Indian, and Turkish silk weavings (see cat. no. 43); Indian and Turkish embroideries; Javanese *batiks* (see cat. no. 55); Kashmiri weavings; rugs and rug fragments (see cat. no. 57); and embroideries and weavings from around the Mediterranean Sea. In addition to Peruvian textiles, Dr. Ross placed in the Museum weavings from Central America, Mexico, and the American Southwest. When a tally of the collection was made in 1902, Dr.

Ross had given over three-fifths of the more than 5,000 textiles then in the collection, and he was to continue his gifts for almost thirty years more.

Due to the accelerated growth of textile acquisitions in the late nineteenth century, plans were made in 1890 to open the Textile Study Room in the Museum, where objects not on exhibition could be seen. In the *Annual Report* for 1897, J. Elliot Cabot, a trustee, described the plans for this facility:

> The [textile] samples are mounted on frames, classified and arranged chronologically and by nationality, so as to be easily accessible. Too numerous for public exhibition, they will be open to students and designers on making previous application. It is confidently believed that a study of these selected examples of design and color must tend to elevate the standard of taste and be of great service to all students of design and to manufacturers, especially of textiles and of paper hangings.[4]

In 1898 this study room was opened to the public, and the first visitors who came to study textiles there "expressed great surprise at the extent, variety and excellence of the collection."[5] Through the years the study facilities became more widely known, and their success is indicated by Samuel D. Warren, president of the board of trustees, in the 1904 *Annual Report*:

> The Collection of Textiles has been enlarged and enriched — most particularly through the liberality of Dr. Denman W. Ross. With students of design, artists and artisans engaged in the textile industries, it is already an influence of real value and usefulness. More liberal exhibition will surely win for it the general recognition it deserves.[6]

The growing use of these holdings required the attention of a full-time staff member, and Jenny Brooks was appointed Assistant in Charge of Textiles in 1900. Conservation of the collection was also begun at this time. In 1905 Emile Bernat began his long association with the Museum with the cleaning and repairing of the recently acquired "Red Sea" tapestry. To help

keep up with the large volume of textile acquisitions entering the collection, Helen Lehr was engaged in 1906 for their mending and mounting.

In 1905 Miss Brooks resigned her appointment, and Sarita G. Flint was named as her successor. Miss Flint worked to make the collection better known not only through exhibitions but also through a series of articles, mainly on recent acquisitions, which were published in the Museum *Bulletin.* To acquaint herself with other notable collections of textiles, she traveled in Europe for sixteen weeks in 1908, during which time she managed the admirable feat of visiting over one hundred museum and private collections. Upon her return, she was able to substantiate the quality of Boston's textile collection based on comparisons with its European counterparts. She wrote that our European tapestry collection was small and laces were still not well represented, although both areas did contain exceptional examples. However, she continued:

> A comparison with these [European] collections shows ours to be richer than most in Persian and Turkish velvets and brocades, and well provided with those of Italian make…. The present standing of the textile collection as a whole gives it a valid claim on the active support of friends of the art in Boston.[7]

In 1910 Miss Flint was granted a second leave of absence to study the landmark exhibition of Mohammedan art in Munich and to visit European museums again. Through her work in Boston and her familiarity with other collections, she came to be recognized as an authority in the field, and in 1920 she was called upon by the Detroit Institute of Arts and the Cleveland Museum of Art to assist in the cataloguing of their textile collections.

Under Miss Flint's direction and with Dr. Ross's enthusiastic support, the Museum continued to add all types of western European textiles to its holdings, including important late medieval Flemish tapestries. Major additions of pre-Columbian Peruvian textiles

4. *Annual Report,* Museum of Fine Arts, Boston, 1897, p. 10.

5. *Annual Report,* Museum of Fine Arts, Boston, 1898, p. 12.

6. *Annual Report,* Museum of Fine Arts, Boston, 1904, p. 21.

7. *Annual Report,* Museum of Fine Arts, Boston, 1908, p. 80.

and Javanese *batiks* were made; William Sturgis Bigelow and others gave large numbers of Japanese and Chinese robes (see cat. no. 51); and Indian textiles of all techniques were acquired.

When the Museum moved to its present location on Huntington Avenue in November 1909, a new textile study room was set up to meet the demands of students and designers. Its popularity was immediate and throughout the 1910s and 1920s it continually brought more people to the Department of Textiles office than visited any other department in the Museum.

Miss Flint resigned her position in 1919, although she remained as an adviser for a brief time, and Gertrude Townsend was appointed Assistant in Charge of Textiles in her place. At that time the textiles were still housed in the Department of Western Arts, which had also included paintings until the establishment of a separate Department of Paintings in 1912. As the Museum's holdings continued to grow, more specialized departments were formally established to care for and make better use of the collections. Thus, in 1926 a Department of Decorative Arts of Europe and America was created, at which time the textiles were placed under its umbrella, with Gertrude Townsend as Keeper. The collections proved too broad and important to remain there for long, however, and the trustees voted to establish formally a separate Department of Textiles as of January 1, 1930, naming Gertrude Townsend as the first Curator of Textiles. By so doing the Boston Museum became the first general art museum in America to place textiles officially on a wholly equal status with the other art forms in its possession.

During these years Miss Townsend continued the series of scholarly articles on new acquisitions in the Museum's *Bulletin,* a practice begun by Miss Flint, and she steadily gained more recognition for the sound art-historical approach she brought to a discipline that was at that time little developed in this country. Miss Townsend was a natural teacher, with a great desire to share whatever knowledge she had gained through her study. Countless laymen and professionals benefited from discussions with her, a fact demonstrated by

the frequency with which she has been acknowledged in print for her assistance.[8]

Miss Townsend made a concerted effort to strengthen those areas of the collection not sufficiently well represented; while the holdings were vast in number, there remained many weak areas. In the field of European tapestries, she recommended in 1926 the purchase of eight fragments from an important fifteenth-century Franco-Flemish series entitled "Stories of Virtuous Women," which had been woven for Cardinal Ferry de Clugny; and in 1929 a remarkable late medieval Flemish tapestry, *Christ Before Pilate and Herod,* came to the Museum as the gift of Robert Treat Paine, 2nd, in memory of his son, Walter Cabot Paine.

Distinguished examples of Islamic textiles were sought out to add to the already considerable holdings in this area, one of the most important coming to the Museum as the gift of Mrs. Walter Scott Fitz: a sixteenth-century Persian velvet weaving depicting hunting scenes (cat. no. 44). Miss Townsend also worked to assemble a notable collection of early European silk weavings, still relatively scarce in American museums today. Many came from European church reliquaries, such as an eighth-century Byzantine fragment from a shroud of Viventia, daughter of Pepin the Short (cat. no. 6); a weaving from Spain, dating from about 1100, which came from a shroud of San Pedro de Osma (cat. no. 7); and a fragment from the shroud of Guy de Lusignon, woven in Italy in the twelfth century (cat. no. 8). Important church vestments were also accessioned through Miss Townsend's efforts, chief among them being a twelfth-century bell-shaped chasuble and a thirteenth-century bishop's cap (miter), both from the Church of Saint Peter in Salzburg (Austria) (cat. nos. 11 and 12).

Among the ever-increasing number of late medieval European tapestry weavings to enter the collection was a Franco-Flemish hanging, *The Martyrdom of Saint Paul,* which had been woven for the Cathedral of Saint Peter in Beauvais (France; cat. no. 10). Since 1934, when the Charles Potter

Kling Fund for the purchase of tapestries and early Italian paintings was established, the Museum has acquired a number of important tapestry weavings that might otherwise have gone elsewhere. Miss Townsend's acquisitions were not limited to western cultures, however; in 1930 the Museum purchased a collection of thirty-seven Indonesian *ikats* from A.J.C. Van Kerckhoff of the Netherlands, who had gathered his collection in a brief period just prior to World War I.

The bulk of these important acquisitions were purchases, since few textiles of this degree of rarity were ever in the hands of collectors in the Boston area. As the supply of textiles in private hands dwindled in the 1930s, Miss Townsend was forced increasingly to look outside New England for potential donors. Simultaneously, it became more difficult to maintain relations with the most prominent textile dealers, who were based in a Europe on the brink of World War II. It was at this time that Miss Townsend met two Americans whose collections, when they ultimately came to the Museum, made its holdings of western embroideries the most comprehensive in this country.

In 1938 Philip Lehman of New York generously gave the Museum his late wife's unique collection of over 350 textiles and costume accessories, which included exquisite examples of professional sixteenth- through eighteenth-century European embroidery (see cat. nos. 18, 39, and 40), unique for their excellent state of preservation. This gift marked the beginning of an effort to build up the Museum's holdings of European embroideries and led to another major acquisition just five years later.

The formidable collection of Elizabeth Day McCormick of Chicago includes embroideries from virtually all parts of the world, a superlative costume collection, and other textiles as well. In 1943 Miss McCormick agreed to give her collection of nearly 5,000 objects to the Boston Museum, surely the most important single gift ever made to the Department of Textiles. While its importance and diversity defy adequate summarization, embroideries, costumes, and costume accessories

8. *Bed Ruggs/1722-1833* (Hartford, 1972), pp. 8-9, contains a frank, affectionate reminiscence written by William Lamson Warren of his visit with Miss Townsend regarding the historical and technical background of American bed rugs and the assistance she offered him.

can be singled out as especially outstanding. Particularly well represented in this group are embroideries from Elizabethan England (cat. nos. 15 and 30). Miss McCormick was enlightened in her agreement to allow the Museum to exchange duplicates and objects of secondary importance from her collection for other objects that would better complement it. In this way, many beautiful textiles have been added to the collection in recent years, one of which is a silk curtain with richly embroidered allegorical scenes (cat. no. 17).

As a result of Miss McCormick's gift, the Boston Museum today possesses one of the foremost collections of costumes in this country, one especially noted for eighteenth-century examples of men's and women's formal dress (see cat. nos. 32 and 33). Accessories of every type were included in her gift, and while it would be difficult to designate one area as more important than another, the 166 examples of footwear in her collection form the best representation of fifteenth-through early twentieth-century shoes in this country (see cat. no. 42).

Several costumes and accessories were already in the Museum prior to Miss McCormick's gift, but they had always been catalogued by their technique, such as "embroidery" or "damask." Now the costume holdings were suddenly so vast that they required treatment as a separate unit within the department. When a large group of Miss McCormick's costumes and accessories were exhibited in the Museum in 1945, great interest was generated in this collection, and many donors have made additions to enrich the holdings since that time. While these gifts have come from many quarters, a few individuals have made especially noteworthy contributions, among them the Misses Aimée and Rosamond Lamb, Mrs. Robert Homans (see cat. no. 35), Mrs. J.D. Cameron Bradley, and Mrs. Edward R. Mitton (see cat. no. 36).

In the late 1930s, Miss Townsend spoke with the chief curator of the Musées Royaux d'Art et d'Histoire, Jean Capart, lamenting the inability of Boston to match that institution's superb collections of tapestries and laces. M. Capart encouraged her to look to her native New England for textiles of distinction that might be the basis for a collection, and it was with this suggestion in mind that Miss Townsend began to trace and record the extant examples of New England domestic embroidery so widely practiced in the eighteenth century. In this search she was aided by Mrs. Samuel Cabot, a long-time friend of and donor to the Department of Textiles. A handful of examples were already in the Museum collection, such as the bed hangings from the Bradstreet family (cat. no. 27) and the "Fishing Lady" embroidered picture (cat. no. 28). Most were still in private hands, however, often within the family of the maker. Together, Miss Townsend and Mrs. Cabot set out to document the whereabouts of these embroideries and organized a loan exhibition of New England needlework pictures at the Museum in 1941. Many of these pictures were subsequently given to the Museum, along with bed hangings, samplers, and other related examples of American embroidery.

Miss Townsend continued to acquire and publish until her retirement in 1959, when Perry T. Rathbone, then director, wrote of her:

> Presiding over this [textile] department for thirty years, Miss Townsend has long been the acknowledged "dean" of American textile curators. Under her guidance, the Boston collection developed into one of the foremost in the world with unexampled concentrations of embroidery, both European and American, Coptic and pre-Columbian textiles, as well as distinguished representations in virtually every field and period of this universal art. The costume collection which Miss Townsend was entirely responsible for forming — and largely through an untold number of gifts — is an *embarras de richesse*. [9]

Happily, Miss Townsend remained closely associated with the Museum after her retirement, and she held the title of curator emerita at the time of her death in the spring of 1979.

Adolph S. Cavallo, who had worked with Miss Townsend as assistant curator, was appointed curator in 1960, a position he retained until his resignation in 1969.[10] He turned increasing

Textile Study Room, 1915 ▷

"New England Needlework to 1800," Textile Gallery, December 20, 1977 – March 5, 1978 ▷

"2500 Years of Peruvian Weaving," Textile Gallery, March 21 – July 11, 1978 ▷

9. *Annual Report,* Museum of Fine Arts, Boston, 1959, p. 2.
10. Mr. Cavallo is at present Curator of Costume and Textiles at the Philadelphia Museum of Art.

energy toward the publication, exhibition, and conservation of the existing collection, which by that time numbered over 25,000 objects. Foremost among Mr. Cavallo's publications for the Museum is the 1967 catalogue *Tapestries of Europe and of Colonial Peru in the Museum of Fine Arts, Boston*. This scholarly two-volume work examines in depth fifty-five of the most important European tapestry hangings and the eleven Colonial Peruvian weavings in the Museum collection at that time. It is organized to give a brief history of tapestry weaving in those two centers, with an introduction explaining the technique and design of European tapestry weavings. Among his other writings are articles on subjects as varied as a carpet made in Cairo around 1500, pre-Columbian Peruvian textiles, and Scottish linen damask weavings.

Of the exhibitions Adolph Cavallo organized, the most memorable was "She Walks in Splendor," staged in 1963. This exhibition featured costumes and accessories from the entire range of the Museum collection, dressed on mannequins especially designed for this installation. The public's interest in the exhibition was great, and again, as a result, many additional costumes were offered as gifts.

In his renovation of the Department of Textiles' spaces in the Museum, Mr. Cavallo established a better-equipped conservation room, improved storage facilities, and flexible galleries for changing exhibitions from the permanent collection. One major consideration in establishing this policy of changing exhibitions, in place of the relatively static ones that had preceded them, was the greater knowledge now available regarding proper preservation techniques for textiles, which are highly susceptible to damage from continuous exposure to light, extremes of humidity, impure air, and stress. A second consideration was the advantage of showing on rotation a much wider selection of the department's varied holdings, thereby creating greater interest in the Museum's total textile collection. This program required skilled work in the preparation of textiles for exhibition and in proper maintenance of the collection, and the Museum was fortunate to acquire for these tasks the services of Mrs. Benjamin A. Markell, who served as conservator of textiles from 1960 until her retirement in 1974.

Mr. Cavallo was responsible for the accession of a remarkable number of key textiles and costumes during his curatorship, acquisitions made both to strengthen parts of the collection that were already substantial and to fill voids. Chief among them are the Cairene carpet referred to above (cat. no. 46); an important group of seventeenth-century Indian textiles given by John Goelet (see cat. nos. 49 and 50); a sixteenth-century Persian hunting carpet that was purchased for the Museum's centennial celebration (cat. no. 48); numerous weavings, including the beautiful *millefleurs* tapestry *Narcissus* (cat. no. 14); and the well-known Afro-American quilt made by Harriet Powers (cat. no. 29). One void was filled in 1965, when Mr. Cavallo recommended the purchase of an outstanding collection of European linen damask weavings (see cat. no. 16). With its acquisition, the Boston Museum now possesses the most comprehensive collection of these weavings in the United States.

In 1969 Larry Salmon was chosen to head the Department of Textiles, which, under his direction, continues to observe the criteria for building up and using the collections established by Miss Townsend and refined by Mr. Cavallo. Since the opening in 1971 of the new textile galleries, the department has installed over thirty different textile and costume exhibitions drawn entirely from the Museum's holdings. These exhibitions have included "Textiles from Egyptian Tombs," "Javanese Batiks," "French Rococo and Neoclassic Textiles," "New England Needlework to 1800," "2,500 Years of Peruvian Weaving," and "The Well-Dressed Eighteenth-Century Man." Many of these exhibitions have been accompanied by gallery guides or other publications.

The preparation of objects for exhibitions requires skilled and devoted work; since Mrs. Markell's retirement, this task has been supervised by Leslie Melville Smith, associate conservator of textiles. To minimize the deteriorating effects of aging and of the elements, Mrs. Smith has conducted diligent research to find new and safer methods of mounting and storing textiles.

Selective acquisitions continue to be made, as diverse as a fourth-century Eastern Mediterranean textile depicting Dionysos (cat. no. 4), an early eighteenth-century "bizarre" silk weaving probably made in France (see cover illustration), and a Peruvian feather panel dating from A.D. 900 to 1476 (cat. no. 61). The department is fortunate to have been able to add to its outstanding collection of costumes and accessories by gift, notably through the generosity of Esther Oldham, who donated her renowned collection of over 400 fans and fan leaves to the Museum in 1976 (see cat. no. 38).

The diverse activities of the Department of Textiles today reflect the long-established goal of making the collections better known to a wide audience, and publications and exhibitions such as "From Fiber to Fine Art" continue to broaden their appeal. Observing the rich variety of textiles and costumes represented here, we are moved to pay homage to those who created them. These artisans possessed an intimate appreciation for the materials with which they worked — wool, silk, linen, and cotton — exploiting to the fullest the potentials of these fibers. The results of their efforts are textiles of such high quality and arresting visual impact that they have secured a firm place among the greatest objects of fine art ever produced.

LARRY SALMON

1

Pan and Dionysos
Eastern Mediterranean, Graeco-Roman,
A.D. 300-400
Wool tapestry weaving
H.: 36 cm. (14¼ in.); w.: 40 cm. (15¾ in.)
Charles Potter Kling Fund. 53.18

Dionysos, here in the company of Pan, is surrounded by various attributes: a pair of castanets, a goat, Pan's pipes, a garland, and a drinking cup. The setting and artistic style of this textile are quite different from those of another representation of Dionysos illustrated here (cat. no. 4). These variations suggest their manufacture in different but contemporary Graeco-Roman weaving centers.

2 (detail)

All dimensions are maximum for the entire object, to the nearest centimeter and quarter-inch.

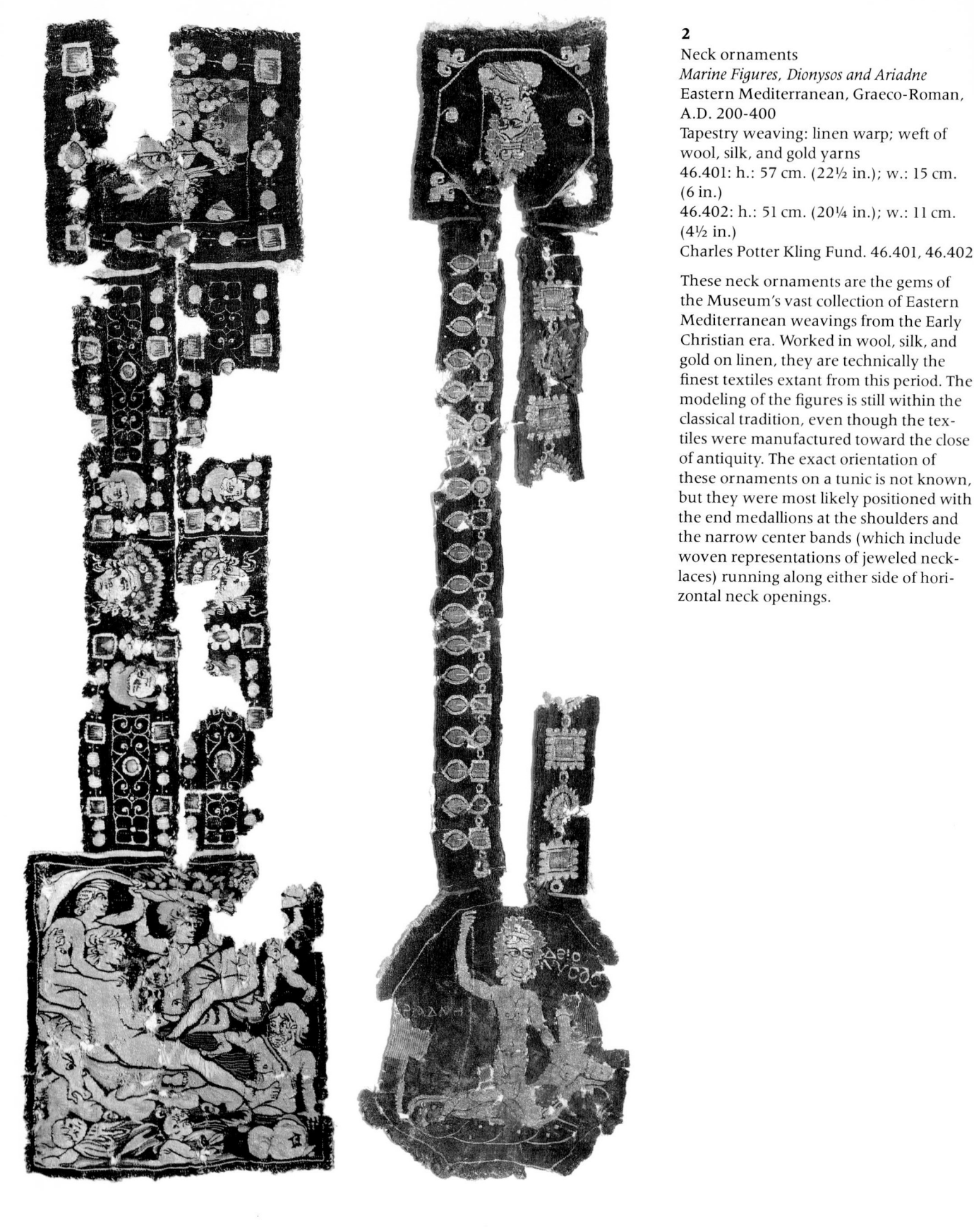

Neck ornaments
Marine Figures, Dionysos and Ariadne
Eastern Mediterranean, Graeco-Roman,
A.D. 200-400
Tapestry weaving: linen warp; weft of
wool, silk, and gold yarns
46.401: h.: 57 cm. (22½ in.); w.: 15 cm.
(6 in.)
46.402: h.: 51 cm. (20¼ in.); w.: 11 cm.
(4½ in.)
Charles Potter Kling Fund. 46.401, 46.402

These neck ornaments are the gems of
the Museum's vast collection of Eastern
Mediterranean weavings from the Early
Christian era. Worked in wool, silk, and
gold on linen, they are technically the
finest textiles extant from this period. The
modeling of the figures is still within the
classical tradition, even though the textiles were manufactured toward the close
of antiquity. The exact orientation of
these ornaments on a tunic is not known,
but they were most likely positioned with
the end medallions at the shoulders and
the narrow center bands (which include
woven representations of jeweled neck-
laces) running along either side of horizontal neck openings.

3
Fragment
Eastern Mediterranean, Graeco-Roman,
probably A.D. 400-500
Compound silk weaving: weft twill
H.: 9 cm. (3½ in.); w.: 7 cm. (2¾ in.)
Ross Collection. 11.90

From 1893 through 1928 Denman W.
Ross gave hundreds of Early Christian
tapestry weavings, which had come from
excavations in Egypt. These textiles,
together with a large group purchased in
1890 from Robert Forrer, an archaeolo-
gist/excavator, today form the nucleus of
the Museum's exceptional collection of
Eastern Mediterranean weavings.
Included in Ross's gifts were rare silk
pieces such as this delicate depiction of a
herdsman surrounded by animals, one of
the earliest compound silk fabrics pre-
served from the Mediterranean area.

4
Wall hanging
Dionysos
Eastern Mediterranean, Graeco-Roman,
A.D. 300-400
Tapestry weaving: linen warp; weft of
wool and linen yarns
H.: 139 cm. (54¾ in.); w.: 79 cm. (31 in.)
Charles Potter Kling Fund. 1973.290

Depicting the god Dionysos seated
beneath a golden niche with a small pan-
ther at his feet, these fragments were
once part of a large wall hanging. Other
known portions of the tapestry are in the
Cleveland Museum of Art and the Abegg-
Stiftung in Riggisberg (Switzerland). This is
the most important Eastern Mediterranean acquisition made by the Boston
Museum throughout the 1960s and 1970s.

5
Fragment
Eastern Mediterranean, Byzantine with
Persian influence, probably A.D. 500-600
Compound silk weaving: weft twill
H.: 31 cm. (12¼ in.); w.: 18 cm. (7¼ in.)
Ross Collection. 04.1620

This weaving features paired birds in
medallions, arranged in a lattice design of
diagonal flowering vines. It is one of a
small number of important early silk
weavings in the collection known to have
been excavated at Antinoë in Egypt.

6
Fragment of a shroud
Byzantium, A.D. 700-800
Compound silk weaving: weft twill
L.: 20 cm. (8 in.); w.: 35 cm. (13¾ in.)
1931 Purchase Fund. 33.648

During her tenure as Curator of Textiles, Gertrude Townsend sought out early medieval European silk weavings for the Museum's collection to complement the several hundred fifteenth- through eighteenth-century silk weavings — velvets, damasks, and brocaded textiles — that had been given to the Museum in the late nineteenth century. Often these early weavings were a part of European church treasuries, as is the case with this shroud and two others illustrated here (cat. nos. 7 and 8). Featuring griffons and leopards in combat, this silk fragment comes from the tomb of Viventia, daughter of Pepin the Short, in the Church of Saint Ursula in Cologne (Germany).

7

Fragment of a shroud
Southern Spain, about 1100
Compound weaving: silk and metallic
yarns
L.: 43 cm. (17 in.); w.: 50 cm. (19¾ in.)
Ellen Page Hall Fund. 33.371

The design of this silk weaving, featuring
harpies and lions in large roundels, is one
of the most intricate and beautiful of the
Middle Ages. For many years the textile
was thought to come from Baghdad, one
of the most famous weaving centers of
the time, and the inscription in the small
roundels identifies that city as its place of
origin. Today, however, the weaving is
attributed to the looms of Islamic weavers
who had settled in southern Spain. It was
entombed with San Pedro de Osma
(d. 1109) in the Cathedral of Burgo de
Osma.

8

Fragments of a shroud
Italy, 1150-1200
Silk double cloth
L.: 53 cm. (21 in.); w.: 32 cm. (12½ in.)
Helen and Alice Colburn Fund. 40.53

The *fleurs-de-lis* of this double cloth are
arranged in chevron bands, separated by
bands of pseudo-Arabic script. The textile
is believed to have been part of the
shroud of Guy de Lusignon (d. 1194),
regent of the kingdom of Jerusalem and
king of Cyprus.

10 ◁

Wall hanging

The Martyrdom of Saint Paul

France or the Franco-Flemish territories,
about 1460

Tapestry weaving: wool warp; weft of
wool, silk, and metallic yarns

H.: 286 cm. (112½ in.); w.: 205 cm.
(80¾ in.)

Francis Bartlett Fund. 38.758

In the Museum's notable collection of
nearly 100 European tapestry weavings,
those of the late middle ages are especially well represented. Of the many
important examples in a good state of
preservation, one of the most outstanding, *The Martyrdom of Saint Paul*, belongs
to a series of tapestries entitled "The Life
of Saint Peter." It was commissioned in
1460 by Guillaume de Hellande (Bishop
of Beauvais from 1444 to 1462) for the
Beauvais Cathedral.

9

Wall hanging

Wild Men and Moors (detail)

South Germany (possibly Strasbourg),
about 1400

Tapestry weaving: linen warp; wool weft

H.: 100 cm. (39¼ in.); w.: 490 cm
(193 in.)

Charles Potter Kling Fund. 54.1431

Acquired by purchase through the
Charles Potter Kling Fund in 1954, this
was the first German tapestry to enter the
Museum's collection. Because of its imaginative design, skillful workmanship, and
excellent condition, it is one of the most
important medieval German tapestry
weavings in existence today. The subject
matter of the hanging, that of wild men
engaged in various pursuits, was a favor-
ite of the medieval traditions in art, literature, and folklore. In the detail illustrated
here, a group of wild men storm a castle
defended by Moors.

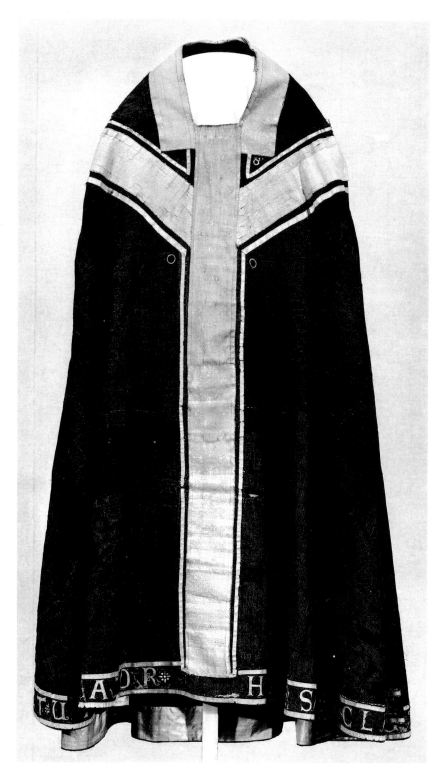

12
Miter
Austria (Salzburg), 1200-1300
Silk and metallic yarns embroidered on silk compound woven ground
Miter: h.: 23 cm. (9 in.); w.: 29 cm. (11½ in.)
Lappets: l.: 48 cm. (19 in.); w.: 6 cm. (2¼ in.)
Helen and Alice Colburn Fund. 38.887

The privilege of wearing a miter, a head-dress worn by bishops and certain abbots, was granted to the abbots of the Church of Saint Peter in Salzburg in 1231. This is an example of the *mitre auriphrygiata,* characterized by gold embroidery on white silk, which could be worn only by abbots exempt from the jurisdiction of a bishop.

11
Chasuble
Sicily or Italy, 1100-1200
Metallic yarns embroidered on silk compound woven ground
L. (center back): 153 cm. (60¼ in.)
Ellen Frances Mason Fund. 33.676

The Boston Museum has a broad collection of western church vestments of all types — copes, chasubles, dalmatics, miters, stoles, maniples, gloves, shoes, etc. — as well as ceremonial garments made for the Greek and the Russian Orthodox churches. This chasuble and a miter (cat. no. 12), both of which came from the Church of Saint Peter in Salzburg (Austria), are among the earliest and most important vestments belonging to the Museum. The origin of the dark silk ground is uncertain, but the gold orphrey strips were probably woven in Sicily. The embroidered Latin inscription at the hem reads "Heinrich, the sinner, completed this noble garment for St. Peter's altar, that it may be his helper." It is the presence of this inscription that most likely assured the preservation of the chasuble in its original full-length bell shape.

13

Wall hanging
The Assumption of the Virgin
Flanders (Brussels), 1530-1535
Tapestry weaving: wool warp; weft of
wool, silk, and metallic yarns
H.: 316 cm. (124½ in.); w.: 205 cm.
(80¾ in.)
Charles Potter Kling Fund. 1975.810

Among the textiles the Boston Athenaeum deposited in the Museum of Fine
Arts in 1876 was this Brussels tapestry. It
is one of a set made for Cardinal Erard de

la Marck, prince-bishop of what is now
the Belgian province of Liège. The com-
position is thought to be copied from an
engraving by the Master of the Die after
Raphael's lost scheme for the altarpiece of
the Chigi Chapel in S. Maria del Popolo in
Rome. In 1975 the Museum purchased
this weaving from the Athenaeum with
the Charles Potter Kling Fund.

14
Wall hanging
Narcissus
France or the Franco-Flemish territories,
1480-1520
Tapestry weaving: wool warp; weft of
wool and silk yarns
H.: 282 cm. (111 in.); w.: 311 cm.
(122½ in.)
Charles Potter Kling Fund. 68.114

Acquired for the Museum's centennial in
1970, this late medieval hanging depicts
Narcissus gazing at his reflection in a
fountain against a *millefleurs* background.
Of all surviving examples of *millefleurs*
tapestries, this is the only one showing a
subject derived from Ovid's *Metamorphoses*.

15 ▷
Part of a long cover
England, 1600-1625
Silk and metallic yarns embroidered on
linen ground
L.: 184 cm. (72½ in.); w.: 76 cm. (30 in.)
The Elizabeth Day McCormick Collection.
43.253

The Museum's collection of sixteenth-
through eighteenth-century English
embroidery is outstanding. It includes
costumes and costume accessories such
as gloves, bags, and stockings, as well as
objects intended for use as household
furnishings, for example, covers, bed
hangings, pictures, samplers, and pillow
slips. The majority of these embroideries,
including this cover, came to the Museum
from 1943 through 1953 as the gift of
Elizabeth Day McCormick.

16
Napkin
Orpheus
Possibly Holland, about 1650
Linen damask weaving
L.: 105 cm. (41½ in.); w.: 74 cm. (29 in.)
Arthur T. Cabot Fund. 65.152

In 1965 the Museum was fortunate to be
able to purchase a collection of Flemish,
Dutch, and German linen damasks of the
late sixteenth to mid-eighteenth century.
The group consists of three tablecloths
and fifty-nine napkins, one of which is
illustrated here. The Museum already had
many such linen damask weavings, and
its holdings are now the most comprehensive in the United States.

17 ▷
Curtain
Possibly Italy, 1675-1725
Silk and metallic yarns embroidered on
silk satin ground
H.: 324 cm. (120 in.); w.: 270 cm.
(106¼ in.)
Purchased for the Elizabeth Day
McCormick Collection. 65.880

Very few embroideries of the superb
workmanship and enchanting design
of this curtain have come down to the
present in such excellent condition.
Among the flowers scattered over the
curtain's surface, Orpheus plays his harp,
real and fantastic animals and birds play,
grotesques recline, and two cupids pull a
ribboned chain of hearts from a fountain
of love. This is but one of the many
objects purchased by exchange for the
Elizabeth Day McCormick Collection.

17 (detail)

18
Hanging pocket case
Probably Italy, 1675-1725
Silk yarns and metallic yarns and wires embroidered on silk; decorated with lace, spangles, painted paper, applied satin, and raised work
H.: 61 cm. (24 in.); w.: 18 cm. (7¼ in.)
Gift of Philip Lehman in memory of his wife, Carrie L. Lehman. 38.1289

Over 350 objects were given the Museum in 1938 by Philip Lehman. Consisting mainly of European embroideries and costume parts and accessories of the sixteenth through the eighteenth century, this collection represents the ultimate in professional workmanship. One of the more unusual objects in the group is this highly decorated hanging pocket case, which held letters or combs and other objects of a woman's *toilette*.

19 ▷
Bed curtain
India (Gujarat, for the English market), 1675-1725
Glazed cotton; painted, mordant- and resist-dyed
H.: 246 cm. (97 in.); w.: 257 cm. (101¼ in.)
Samuel Putnam Avery Fund and Gift of Mrs. Samuel Cabot. 53.2201

This glazed painted cotton or chintz, made in India for the European market, is part of a set of bed hangings from Ashburnham Place, Sussex, England. The technique used is the same as that of Indian textiles intended for the Mughal court (see cat. no. 50), but the pattern was supplied from Europe, incorporating fashionable chinoiserie elements of the time. An English crewel-embroidered bed curtain fragment with a landscape design identical to that of this chintz is in the Museum's Elizabeth Day McCormick Collection (acc. no. 53.172). The Department of Textiles has a number of good examples of these Indian trade goods, as well as important embroidered bedcovers from British and Portuguese centers in India, also made for export to Europe.

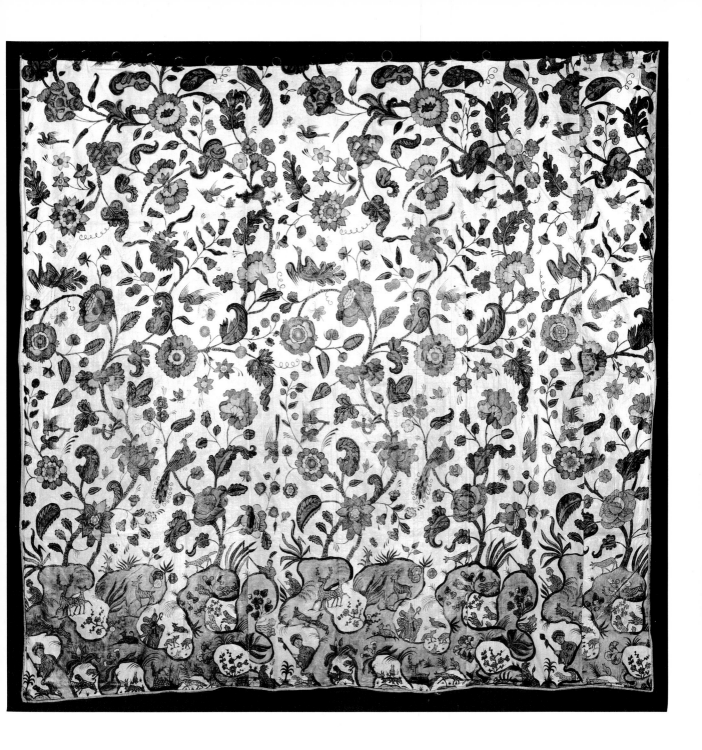

20

Wall hanging
Victoria
Designed by Ludwig Van Schoor and
Pieter Spierinckx, possibly woven by
Josse de Vos
Flanders (probably Brussels), 1700-1725
Tapestry weaving: wool warp; weft of
wool, silk, and metallic yarns
H.: 355 cm. (139¾ in.); w.: 406 cm.
(160 in.)
Gift of Miss Ida Deacon. 71.1

Victoria was the first textile acquired by
the Museum. Given by Ida Deacon in
1871, this tapestry was the second object
to enter the permanent collection (the
first being a painting by Washington
Allston, *Elijah in the Desert).* The central
figure is an allegorical representation of
Victory, surrounded by attendants and
piles of armor and by a woman represent-
ing Peace, who offers her a crown of
leaves. Two captives are seated at the
lower right corner of the tapestry.

21 ▷

Panel
Pastoral scenes (detail)
Designed by Jean-Baptiste Huet
France (Jouy-en-Josas), about 1785-1790
Printed cotton
L.: 250 cm. (98¼ in.); w.: 93 cm.
(36¾ in.)
Gift of Mrs. Samuel Cabot. 44.685a

Cotton printing in Europe developed in
response to the popularity of painted cottons coming out of India (see cat. no. 19,
for example). The Museum has a large
collection of these eighteenth- and nineteenth-century European printed cottons,
many of which have designs based on
contemporary prints. The donor of this
piece, Mrs. Samuel Cabot, pioneered
research in identifying the print sources
for many textile designs and discovered
two engravings by Claudine Bouzonnet
Stella *(The Seesaw* and *After the Wolf!,* after
Jacques Stella) to be the origin of this
pattern.

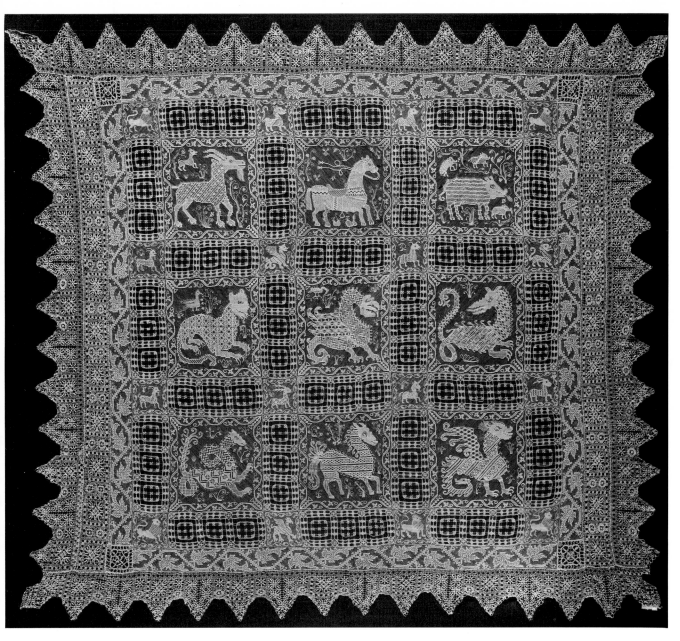

22 (top)
Border (detail)
Italy, 1550-1600
Cut work with needle lace *(reticella)*,
linen yarns
L.: 81 cm. (32 in.); w.: 13 cm. (5 in.)
Bequest of Mrs. Arthur Croft. 01.6308

23 (top)
Border (detail)
Probably Italy, 1575-1625
Bobbin lace, linen yarns
L.: 220 cm. (86¾ in.); w.: 16 cm. (6¾ in.)
Bequest of J.W. Paige. 95.955

The Museum's large collection of six-
teenth- to nineteenth-century European
needle and bobbin laces was one of the
first areas of textiles to be built up. This
was due principally to gifts made in the
nineteenth century by two donors, Mrs.
George W. Wales and J.W. Paige (see also
cat. nos. 24 and 25). Important gifts of
lace have enlarged the collection since
that time, and today the Museum's holdings of lace are both extensive and
representative.

◁ **24**
Woman's headwear (lappet ends; detail)
Germany or Denmark, 1750-1800
Drawn work, linen yarns
L.: 125 cm. (49¼ in.); w.: 9 cm. (3½ in.)
Gift of Mrs. George W. Wales. 82.40

◁ **25**
Woman's headwear (lappet; detail)
France or Flanders, 1725-1750
Bobbin lace with net ground and linen
yarns
L.: 166 cm. (65¼ in.); w.: 12 cm. (4¾ in.)
Bequest of J.W. Paige. 95.875

26
Table cover
Spain, 1550-1650
Darned filet with bobbin lace inserts,
linen yarns
H.: 132 cm. (51¾ in.); w.: 149 cm.
(58¾ in.)
Mary L. Smith Fund. 60.1461

This unique table cover, purchased in
1960, is one of the few laces in the
Museum not acquired by gift. The design
is distinguished by its depiction of diverse,
highly patterned animals, including a
goat, a horse, a lion, a dragon, and many
others.

27
Bed furnishings (four curtains and three valances)
New England (Massachusetts, Boston area), 1700-1750
Wool yarns (crewels) embroidered on cotton and linen twill ground (fustian)
H. (of curtains): 225 cm. (88½ in.)
Gift of Samuel Bradstreet. 19.67, 19.596, 19.597, 19.598, 19.609a-c

The Museum has a large collection of American embroideries, especially strong in objects worked in colonial New England. Among the prizes of this group are the crewel-embroidered bed furnishings that were so popular in the first half of the eighteenth century. This complete set of hangings, worked by a member of the Bradstreet family, had been remade into a bedcover and three wall panels when it came to the Museum. The set was reconstructed in 1971 by the textile conservation staff.

28 ▷
Embroidered picture
The Fishing Lady
Worked by the wife of Col. Sylvanus Bourne
New England, 1740-1760
Wool, silk and metallic yarns, beads, and spangles embroidered on linen canvas
H.: 53 cm. (21 in.); w.: 111 cm. (43¾ in.)
Seth K. Sweetser Fund. 21.2233

The Fishing Lady is one of the most important and well known of the Museum's many American canvaswork pictures. Popular scenes of courtship — a fishing

lady and her escort, a spinning lady and shepherd, and a picnicking couple – are depicted within a bucolic landscape. Tradition has associated the locale of this embroidery with the Boston Common, but it is highly unlikely that any specific representation was intended by the young woman who created it.

29
HARRIET POWERS (American, 1837-1911)
Pictorial quilt
United States (Athens, Georgia), about 1895-1898
Pieced and appliquéd cotton embroidered with cotton and metallic yarns
H.: 175 cm. (69 in.); w.: 267 cm. (105 in.)
M. and M. Karolik Collection. 64.619

The Museum has a small, select collection of American bedcovers, both woven and quilted. Perhaps the most famous of this group is the quilted cover worked by a

black woman, Harriet Powers, in the late nineteenth century, the fifteen squares of which depict biblical tales, localized legends, and astronomical occurrences. The appliqué technique and design motifs used by Mrs. Powers relate to those of textiles made in the African country of Dahomey. Her imaginative conception secures for the quilt a place among the best examples of Afro-American art.

30
Woman's waistcoat and coif
England, 1575-1610
Linen embroidered with metallic yarns
and spangles, trimmed with metallic lace
L. (center back): 43 cm. (17 in.)
The Elizabeth Day McCormick Collection.
43.243, 43.244a

These costume parts, among the most
important in the McCormick collection,
are said to have been given to the wife of
Roger Woodhouse by Queen Elizabeth I
on August 22, 1578. The metallic yarns
are skillfully embroidered to form a raised
pattern of daffodils enclosed by scrolling
stems.

31
Woman's formal dress
Italy or France, 1750-1775
Silk taffeta with supplementary pattern
wefts of silk and metallic yarns, trimmed
with silk flowers and metallic lace
L. (center back): 156 cm. (61½ in.)
Gift of Alessandro Castellani. 77.6a,b

Acquired by gift in 1877, this was the first
costume to enter the Museum of Fine
Arts, and it is still one of the most sump-
tuous gowns in the collection. Until the
1940s, when quantities of costume mate-

rial were given by Elizabeth Day McCormick, the few costumes accessioned were
catalogued according to the technique in
which the fabric was worked—painted
silk, damask, etc. This dress was originally
considered, therefore, as part of the holdings in European silk weavings rather
than as a costume. The new classifications
better define the material, making it more
accessible for study.

32
Woman's formal dress
France, 1760-1780
Painted silk taffeta (from China)
L. (center back): 163 cm. (64½ in.)
The Elizabeth Day McCormick Collection.
43.1633a-d

The silk fabric of this formal dress was made and painted in China, then exported to Europe to be made up as a dress. The Elizabeth Day McCormick Collection, augmented by additional gifts, makes the Museum's holdings of eighteenth-century costume among the most comprehensive in the United States.

33
Man's dress suit
France, 1770-1780
Silk yarns embroidered on silk satin
L. (coat, center back): 106 cm. (41¾ in.)
The Elizabeth Day McCormick Collection.
43.1667a,b; 43.1669c

The silk embroidery of the coat and breeches is worked entirely in minute chain stitches in a delicate floral pattern. Its high quality is typical of the best formal wear of the time.

34
Formal dress
France, about 1800
Cotton and wool yarns embroidered on
cotton gauze
L. (center back): 235 cm. (92½ in.)
Gift of Miss Eleanora Curtis. 22.665

Slippers
Staton, England (London), about 1800
Painted kid uppers, leather soles
L.: 21 cm. (8¼ in.)
Gift of Miss Eleanora Curtis. 22.666a,b

The first costume dating around 1800 to
enter the collection, this dress and pair of
slippers vividly express the classical taste
of that period. Grecian influence may be
seen in the draped silhouette with a high
waistline, highlighted by the red and
white embroidered laurel sprigs and
branches and key-patterned borders. Due
to these unusual embroidered classical
motifs, this dress remains one of the
Museum's most important examples of its
period.

35

MME. ROGER (French)
Ball dress
France (Paris), 1858-1860
Silk taffeta with supplementary pattern
weft, trimmed with tulle, satin, and
blonde lace
L. of bodice (center back): 21 cm. (8¼ in.)
L. of skirt (center back): 176 cm. (69¼ in.)
Gift of Mrs. Robert Homans. 46.207a,b

No other dress in the collection suggests
so well the grace and elegance of fashionable Parisian women of the 1850s and
1860s. The gown was designed by
Mme. Roger, a contemporary of Charles
Frederick Worth and a noted dressmaker
of her time. Her color scheme, white
highlighted with orange and black, is
uncommon for the period. The great
dome shape is achieved by wearing the
skirt over a wide artificial crinoline or
hoop skirt. The unusual design of the
skirt contrasts flounces of tulle in the
front, typical of the skirts of the period,
with large taffeta puffs and a train at the
back, which anticipate the development
of the bustle in the late 1860s. Above the
bulk of the skirt is a delicate bodice,
drawn into a tiny waist.

With the addition of the McCormick collection after 1943, the department began
to build a representative collection of costumes. Among the first major contributions were eleven gowns worn by Fanny
Crowninshield (Mrs. John Quincy)
Adams, given by her daughter. Two of
these dresses were designed by Mme.
Roger and date from 1858-1860, while
the remaining nine came from the House
of Worth and date from 1880-1895.

36
LUCILE (LADY DUFF-GORDON)
(English, 1864-1935)
Evening dress
France (Paris), about 1911
Jet beads, sequins, and rhinestones
embroidered on silk satin and net
trimmed with lace
L. (center back): 128 cm. (50½ in.)
Gift of Mrs. Edward R. Mitton. 54.812

Costume designers in the early years of
this century returned to the high-waisted
columnar silhouette of a century before,
but with a low and prominent bustline.
In contrast to the simple classical garments of the early 1800s, these dresses
often exhibited a complex layered struc-
ture with overlappings and irregular
hemlines, incorporating plain and decorated fabrics of differing textures and
weights, as on the evening dress shown
here. It was designed by Lucile (Lady
Duff-Gordon), the first English dressmaker to win an international reputation.

This evening dress is one of a group of
sixteen worn by Anne Marie Richardson
(Mrs. George W.) Mitton of Boston and
donated to the Museum by her daughter-
in-law. They constitute the finest single
group of costumes from the period 1910-
1930 in the collection.

37
JEANNE LANVIN (French, 1867-1946)
Court presentation gown
France (Paris), 1931
Silk satin
L. of dress (center back): 133 cm.
(52½ in.)
L. of train (center back): 155 cm. (61 in.)
Gift of Mrs. Frederick W. Hilles. 53.415a,b

Prince of Wales's Plume and veil
England (London), 1931
Ostrich feathers and tulle
L.: 146 cm. (57½ in.)
Gift of Mrs. Frederick W. Hilles 53.416

Fan
France, 1931
Ostrich feathers on mother-of-pearl sticks
L.: 64 cm. (25½ in.)
Gift of Mrs. Frederick W. Hilles. 53.417

The tightly fitted and draped silhouette of evening dresses in the 1930s is strikingly illustrated by Parisian designer Jeanne

Lanvin in this court presentation gown of 1931, worn by the donor. To achieve this look, Lanvin used silk satin cut on the bias (diagonal) so that it falls in a smooth vertical drape and clings to the body. With the dress and matching court train, the requisite Prince of Wales's Plume and veil was worn. The wearer also carried a large ostrich feather fan matching the color of the dress.

The Museum's collection contains four gowns worn for presentation at the English court, ranging in date from 1865 to 1931.

38
Mask fan
England (for the Spanish market),
1740-1760
Printed and painted vellum leaf on
painted ivory sticks
L.: 26 cm. (10¼ in.)
Oldham Collection. 1976.179

Cut or *découpé* fan
France, about 1590
Vellum leaf with bits of mica on ivory
sticks
L.: 30 cm. (11¾ in.)
Oldham Collection. 1976.182

The Oldham collection, one of the
world's great collections of fans, was
donated to the Museum in 1976. It
includes 431 fans and fan leaves from
many cultures dating from the sixteenth
to the twentieth century and is especially
strong in eighteenth- and nineteenth-

century European examples. The two
fans illustrated here are an indication of
the high quality of this renowned
collection.

39

Woman's stomacher
France or Italy, 1675-1725
Metallic yarns and wires embroidered on
silk ground
H.: 42 cm. (16½ in.); w.: 31 cm. (12¼ in.)
Gift of Philip Lehman in memory of his
wife, Carrie L. Lehman. 38.1342

Professionally embroidered costume parts
and accessories from the Lehman collection give an idea of the richness of orna-
mentation available to the upper classes
in sixteenth- through eighteenth-century
Europe. This stomacher and a man's cap
(cat. no. 40) are representative of the
collection's uniformly high quality and
excellent state of preservation.

40

Man's negligee cap
Italy, 1675-1725
Metallic yarns and tassels embroidered
on silk cut-velvet ground
H.: 19 cm. (7½ in.)
Gift of Philip Lehman in memory of his
wife, Carrie L. Lehman. 38.1298

41 ▷

Woman's stocking
Germany (Chemnitz), 1900-1917
Cotton lisle knit, printed
L. of foot: 21 cm. (8¼ in.), l. of leg: 81 cm.
(31¾ in.)
The Arthur Warren Rayner Hosiery
Collection
Gift of Mrs. Frank K. Idell. 69.1347

Woman's stocking
Germany (Chemnitz), 1910-1917
Cotton lisle knit, embroidered with silk
L. of foot: 23 cm. (9 in.), l. of leg: 70 cm.
(27½ in.)
The Arthur Warren Rayner Hosiery
Collection
Gift of Mrs. Frank K. Idell. 69.1341a

Woman's stocking
Germany (Chemnitz), 1910-1917
Cotton lisle knit, printed
L. of foot: 24 cm. (9½ in.), l. of leg:
64 cm. (25¼ in.)
The Arthur Warren Rayner Hosiery
Collection
Gift of Mrs. Frank K. Idell. 69.685a

Arthur Warren Rayner collected examples of fashionable hosiery during the
years 1900-1940, while employed by the
dry goods firm of Walker-Stetson Co. of
Boston. This vast collection of 551 examples is a document of hosiery fashion of
the early twentieth century. Many of
those dating from before World War I, like
the three stockings shown here, were
manufactured in Chemnitz, Saxony, Germany, where the highest quality hosiery
was produced.

42

Woman's shoe
Italy, about 1750
Figured silk upper and heel brocaded
with silk and metallic yarns and bobbin
lace (buckle missing); leather sole
L.: 23 cm. (9 in.)
The Elizabeth Day McCormick Collection.
44.488a

Woman's shoe with clog
France, 1625-1675
Leather and silk upper, heel and clog with
applied straw; leather sole
L.: 18 cm. (7 in.)
The Elizabeth Day McCormick Collection.
44.506a

Chopine
Italy (Venice), 1550-1650
Stamped leather mule with silk tassels;
leather-covered cork chopine trimmed
with metallic galloon
L.: 17 cm. (6¾ in.)
The Elizabeth Day McCormick Collection.
44.556a

Outstanding in the McCormick collection
is the European footwear dating from the
sixteenth through eighteenth century,
of which three examples are illustrated
here. This group, originally collected by a
Signor Simonetti in Rome and purchased
by McCormick in the late 1920s, forms
the most extensive collection of its kind in
the United States today.

43
Panel for clothing or furnishing
Turkey or Italy, 1500-1600
Cut and voided silk velvet with supplementary pattern wefts of silk and metallic yarns
L.: 157 cm. (51¾ in.); w.: 64 cm. (25¼ in.)
Ross Collection. 97.467

A great variety of Turkish and Persian silk weavings and embroideries were accessioned by the Museum in its early decades, many coming as the gift of Denman Waldo Ross. This velvet weaving has a striking design that varies in many details from sixteenth-century Turkish weavings, which may indicate that it was made in Turkey for export to Europe or perhaps even woven in an Italian center from Near Eastern models.

44 ▷
Lining for the interior of a tent ceiling
Persia (Safavid), 1525-1550
Cut and voided silk velvet with supplementary pattern weft of metallic wires
D.: 98 cm. (38½ in.)
Gift of Mrs. Walter Scott Fitz. 28.13

Throughout Gertrude Townsend's years on the Museum's professional staff (1919-1960) she worked to add key pieces to the collections of Islamic textiles. Two such examples of these acquisitions are this velvet weaving with hunting scenes and a small double-cloth fragment depicting men in boats (cat. no. 45). This circular panel was used as the lining for the interior of a tent ceiling. It is said to have been captured by the Ottoman Sultan Sulayman the Magnificent during one of his invasions of Persia between 1543 and 1545. It then belonged to Kara Mustapha Pasha, from whom it passed to the hands of a Polish general at the rout of the Turks at Vienna in 1683. This velvet is the most complex Persian silk weaving known, remarkable for the curvilinearity of the drawing, the subtlety of the pattern repeat, and the great number of colors employed.

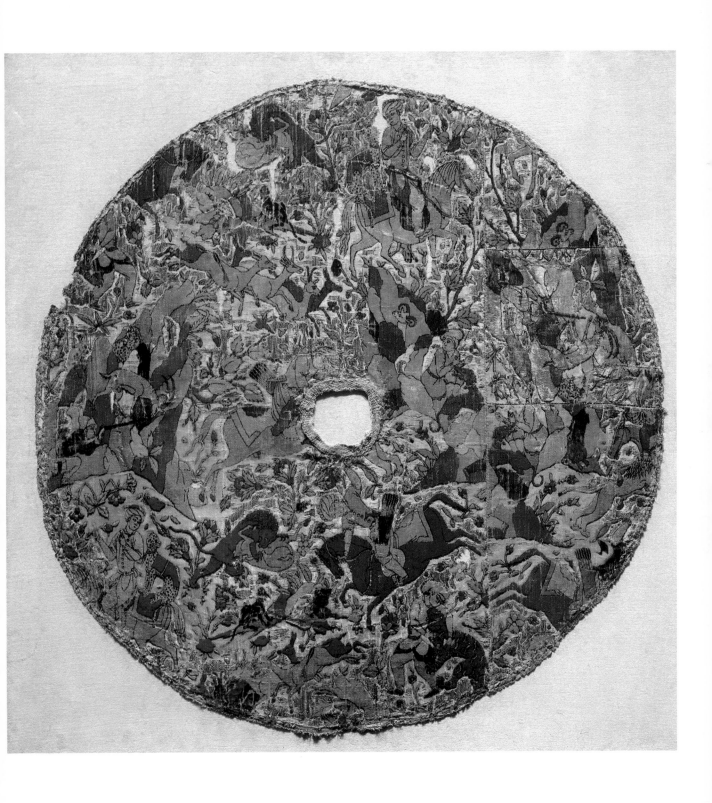

45
Fragment
Persia (Safavid), 1550-1600
Double cloth, silk and metallic yarns
H.: 16 cm. (6¼ in.); w.: 15 cm. (5¾ in.)
H.E. Bolles Fund. 39.296

46
Carpet
Egypt (Cairo; Mamluk), about 1500
Knotted wool pile (Senna knot), wool
warp and weft
L. (excluding fringe): 254 cm. (100 in.);
w.: 279 cm. (110 in.)
Helen and Alice Colburn Fund and
Harriet Otis Cruft Fund. 61.939

The Museum's collection of carpets and
rugs is quite small, with less than 100
examples. Efforts to acquire in this area
have been directed toward obtaining carpets of major significance (cat. nos. 47
and 48, for example), rather than toward
building up a comprehensive collection.
This Cairene carpet, acquired by purchase
in 1961, is a good example of such a collecting philosophy. The luster of its blue,
red, and lime green wool pile gleams like
silk, and its astonishingly good condition
is not equaled by that of any other
example.

46

47
Carpet
India (Mughal), about 1600
Knotted wool pile (Senna knot), cotton
warp and weft
L.: 243 cm. (95¾ in.); w.: 154 cm.
(60¾ in.)
Gift of Mrs. Frederick L. Ames in the
name of Frederick L. Ames. 93.1480

The high degree of pictorial representation in this carpet, derived from Mughal
Indian miniature painting, is unique.
Interspersed with plants and animals are
mythological beasts and realistic scenes of
the hunt and domestic activity.

48
Hunting carpet (details)
Persia (Safavid), 1525-1550
Knotted silk pile (Senna knot), silk warp
and weft, supplementary pattern weft of
metallic yarns
L.: 480 cm. (189 in.); w.: 255 cm.
(100½ in.)
Gift of John Goelet, Centennial Purchase
Fund, and restricted funds. 66.293

The most important carpet in the
Museum's collection is this sixteenth-
century Persian example, one of the great
masterpieces from the royal looms of the
Safavid ruler Shah Tahmasp (1524-1576).
Formerly owned by Baron Maurice de
Rothschild, it was acquired in 1966 for the
Museum's centennial. The large size, the
use of silk throughout, the remarkable
workmanship (up to 810 knots to the
square inch), and the depiction of the
court pastimes of feasting and the hunt all
point to its having been a royal commis-
sion. The several hunting scenes shown
in the field give the carpet its name.

48 (detail)

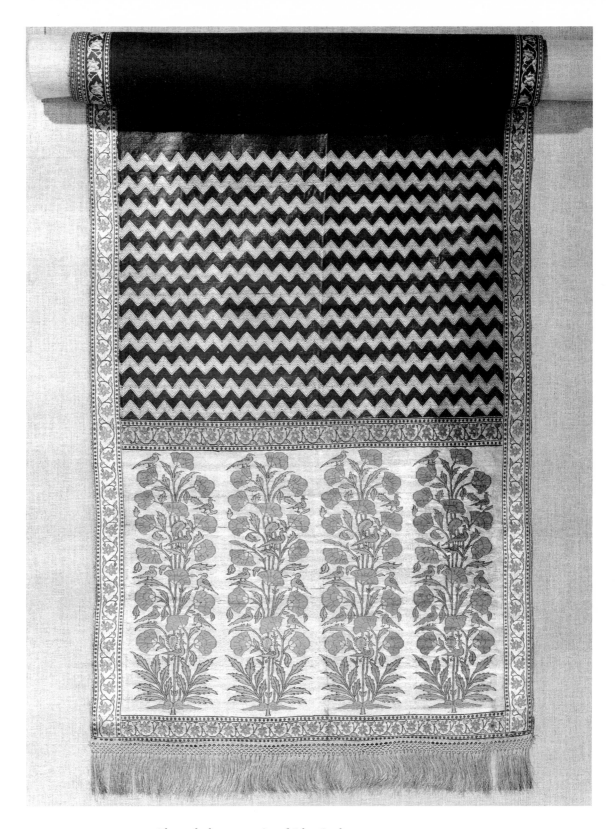

49
Sash *(patka;* detail)
India (Mughal), 1630-1700
Silk twill ground with supplementary
pattern wefts of silk and metallic yarns
L. (excluding fringe): 416 cm. (163¾ in.);
w.: 51 cm. (20 in.)
Gift of John Goelet. 66.858

Through the generosity of John Goelet,
the Museum acquired in 1966 a number
of important Indian textiles from the
Nasli and Alice Heeramaneck Collection.
Combined with the several hundred
already in the Museum, they make this
institution's collection of Indian textiles
one of the most comprehensive in the
world. Sashes such as this are worked in a
variety of techniques, for example, silk
weaving, embroidery, and printed cotton.
They were made primarily for members
of the Mughal court.

50
Small cover
India (Golconda), 1630-1700
Cotton; painted, mordant- and resist-
dyed
H.: 67 cm. (26½ in.); w.: 82 cm.
(32¼ in.)
Gift of John Goelet. 66.230

The technique of cotton painting is an
extremely slow and complicated one,
involving careful treatment with mor-
dants and resist mediums, followed by
immersion in dye baths. Golconda court
workshops were especially famous for
the glowing quality of their reds, ranging
in all shades from pink to purple. This
cover, made at the apex of a 2,000-year
tradition of cotton painting in India, is
one of the most beautiful ever produced.

51 ▷
Nō costume
Japan, Edo Period, 1775-1800
Compound weaving of silk and metallic
yarns with supplementary silk pattern
wefts *(atsuita karaori)*
L. (center back): 143 cm. (56¼ in.)
Gift of William Sturgis Bigelow. 15.1157

In costumes of the *Nō* theater, the motifs
used are most often naturalistic, chiefly
floral. Here five-petaled flowers are set
against a background of red and green
diamond-shaped lattice. Known as *atsuita
karaori,* this type of *Nō* costume is the
major outer robe for women's roles.

The Museum holds the largest and finest
collection of Japanese *Nō* robes outside
Japan. The collection was well established
prior to 1920 through major gifts, chiefly
from Dr. William Sturgis Bigelow.

52
Album leaf
Bird Perching on a Branch of Cherry
China, Southern Sung Period, 1150-1200
Silk tapestry weaving *(kossu)*
H.: 25 cm. (10 in.); w.: 29 cm. (11½ in.)
Chinese and Japanese Special Fund.
37.303

The Museum has a small collection of
Chinese textiles of very high quality, most
important being tapestry weavings in the
form of album leaves. The Southern Sung
example is the finest of its type, and it is
the first leaf in an important album of
Sung and Yüan paintings, also in the
Museum's collection. The Ming example
(cat. no. 53) is based upon Southern
Sung original paintings.

53
Album leaf
Fish and Water Grass
China, Ming Dynasty, about 1550
Silk tapestry weaving *(kossu)*
H.: 26 cm. (10¼ in.); w.: 27 cm. (10¾ in.)
Ross Collection. 17.612

54 ▷
Ceremonial textile *(palepai)*
Indonesia (Sumatra, southern Lampong
region), 1825-1875
Cotton ground with supplementary pat-
tern wefts of cotton and silk yarns
L.: 382 cm. (150½ in.); w.: 74 cm. (29 in.)
William E. Nickerson Fund, No. 2.
1980.172

An outstanding acquisition of 1980 is this
ceremonial cloth of Sumatra, often called
a "ship cloth" in the West after its major
motif. Earlier literature labeled these
motifs "ships of the dead," but their
broader significance is now recognized as
a metaphor for society and its ceremonial
transitions.

The Museum possesses approximately
seventy *ikats* and weavings from eleven
islands of the Indonesian archipelago, in
addition to Javanese *batiks* (see cat. no.
55). Acquired primarily in the 1920s and
1930s, they include thirty-seven examples purchased from the collection of
A.J.C. Van Kerckhoff of the Netherlands.

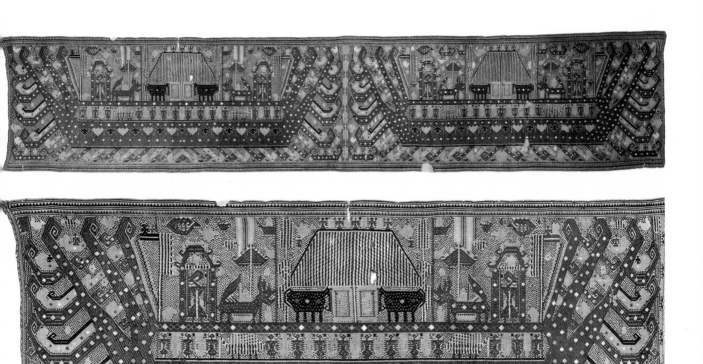

54 (detail)

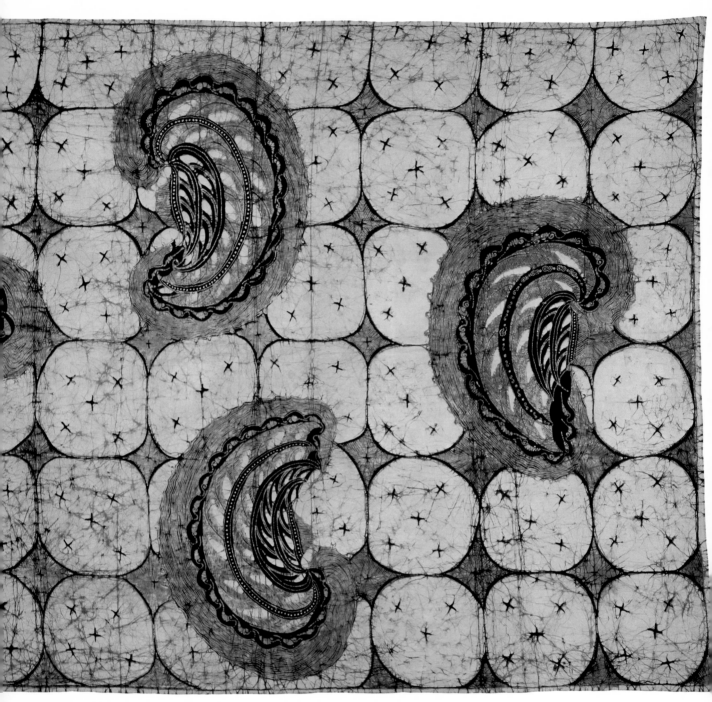

55
Skirt cloth *(kain pandjang;* detail)
Indonesia (Central Java), about 1900
Cotton *batik* (resist-dyed)
L.: 256 cm. (101 in.); w.: 107 cm. (42 in.)
Ross Collection. 11.1344

Denman Ross collected the first *batiks* for
the Museum at the Chicago Exposition of
1893. Through Ross and Dr. Ananda K.
Coomaraswamy, major groups were
added in 1911 and 1921, respectively, with
occasional additions since then. Unique
within the collection of 275 *batiks,* mostly
from Central Java, are 158 design samples
from the court of Surakarta (Solo). They
were purchased by Dr. Coomaraswamy
in 1921 from the private collection of
Prince Ario Kusumodiningrat, brother of
the then-reigning sultan of Surakarta.

56 (detail)

56
Doorway of a bed tent
Greece (Dodecanese Islands, Cos), probably 1700-1800
Silk yarns embroidered on linen ground
H.: 330 cm. (130 in.); w.: 257 cm. (101 in.)
Gift of Mrs. Solomon R. Guggenheim.
50.2625

The Museum's Greek islands and mainland embroidery collection was begun early, the first embroidery being given by Denman Ross in 1883, and the first costume by Louise Nathurst in 1894. The collection was greatly enlarged from 1943 to 1953 through major gifts from the Elizabeth Day McCormick Collection and now numbers approximately 150 costumes and accessories and a variety of decorated household linens. One of the more recent gifts is this outstanding Dodecanese embroidered doorway for a nuptial bed.

57 ▷
Rug (detail)
Western Turkestan, Tekke tribe,
1800-1850
Knotted wool pile (Senna knot), wool warp and weft
L. (excluding fringe): 290 cm. (114¼ in.); w.: 206 cm. (81 in.)
Ross Collection. 09.359

The textile traditions of Western Turkestan are represented in the Museum collection by costumes (see cat. no. 58), embroideries, *ikats,* and woven-pile weavings. This rug or nomadic tent furnishing of the Tekke tribe has a flattened octagon as its major motif and a cruciform diamond as the minor motif. In the field, the octagons are intersected by vertical and horizontal lines.

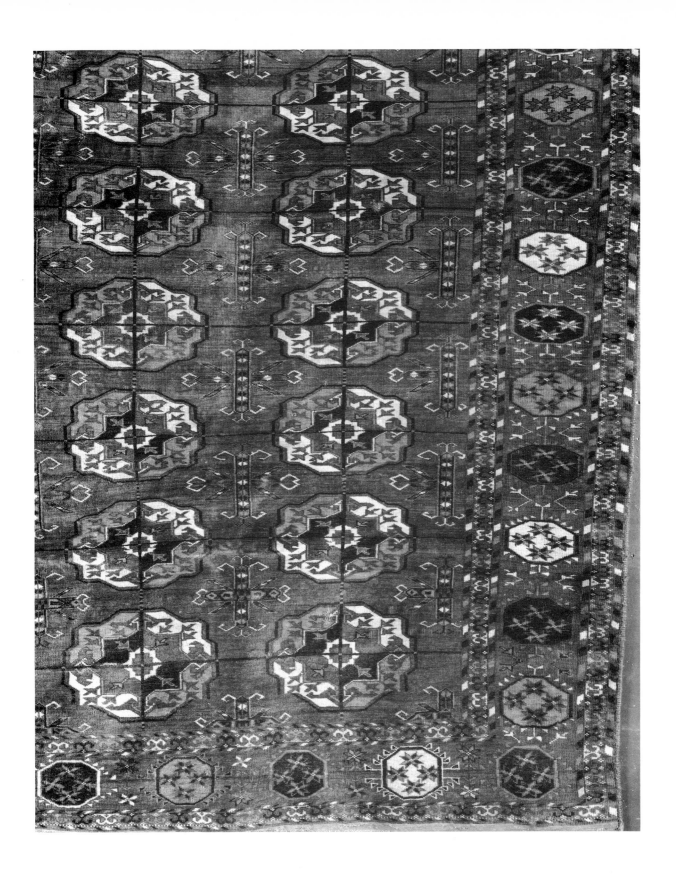

58
Woman's coat *(chalat)*
Western Turkestan, 1800-1900
Silk velvet *ikat* (warp-dyed)
L. (center back): 118 cm. (46½ in.)
Gift in memory of Jay Abrams. 58.342

The elegance of this silk velvet coat is
heightened by the elaborate warp *ikat*
pattern, created by dyeing the warp
yarns prior to weaving the fabric.

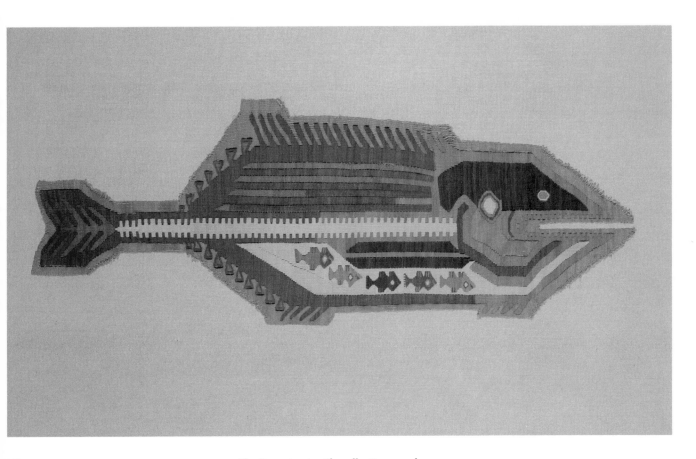

59

Fish

Peru (south coast), probably Late Intermediate Period (900-1476)

Tapestry weaving: cotton warp; wool weft

H.: 18 cm. (7 in.); w.: 49 cm. (19¼ in.)

Harriet Otis Cruft Fund. 31.710

The Peruvian textile collection was begun prior to 1900 with gifts of Edward W. Hooper and Denman Ross. Numbering approximately 300 textiles today, it represents a 2,500-year tradition dating from about 500 B.C. through the Spanish Colonial period. The collection is especially strong in tapestry weaving and embroidery; it also includes double cloth, gauze, painted cotton, and network (see also cat. nos. 60, 61, and 62).

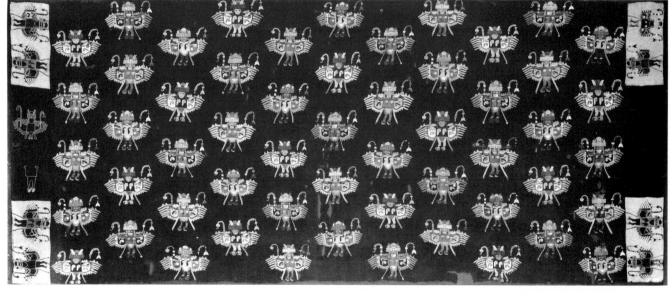

60
Burial mantle
Peru (Paracas), Early Intermediate Period,
Epoch 2 (possibly 300-200 B.C.)
Wool yarns embroidered on wool ground
H.: 102 cm. (40 in.); w.: 247 cm.
(97½ in.)
Ross Collection. 16.34a

Among the most intriguing and rare pre-
Columbian Peruvian textiles are those
from the Paracas peninsula, dating from
approximately 500-200 B.C. Although
the discovery of textiles at this site was
not formally announced until 1925, the
Museum received several of these
embroideries as the gift of Denman Waldo
Ross in 1916. The collection of Paracas
textiles grew significantly with a second
major gift from Ross in 1921 and the purchase of others in 1931. Today the
Museum's holdings of Paracas textiles,

second only to that of the Brooklyn
Museum outside of Peru, numbers almost
fifty examples and includes seven
mantles.

60 (detail)

61
Feather panel
Peru (south coast), probably Late Inter-
mediate Period (900-1476)
Feathers applied to cotton ground
H.: 127 cm. (50 in.); w.: 93 cm. (36½ in.)
Arthur T. Cabot Fund. 1971.76

In pre-Columbian Peru feathers in natural brilliant colors were brought from
birds of the tropical rain forests of the
Amazon region to the south coast for
application to ceremonial textiles. In
addition to this panel, the Museum is
fortunate to have one partial (acc. no.
60.253) and one complete (acc. no.
66.905) feather poncho, all of which
were acquired after 1960.